Old BLAIRGOWRIE and RATTR

by
Maurice Fleming

A summer's day in the Public Park off Perth Road, now covered by the Altamount housing estate. On the left of the picture the tops of the swings are just visible – they stood in a deep sandpit where I and others spent many a happy hour. The park had three entrances – by what is now Queen's Avenue on Perth Road, from the top of Emma Street, and by a footpath from Beeches Road. A small play area survives in a corner of the estate.

© Maurice Fleming, 1997
First Published in the United Kingdom, 1997
By Stenlake Publishing, Ochiltree Sawmill, The Lade,
Ochiltree, Ayrshire KA18 2NX
Telephone/Fax: 01290 423114

ISBN 1 84033 008 2

This was my class picture one year in the late 1930s (I'm third from the right in the front row). There are 50 pupils here – that was the average size of class throughout my primary education at Blairgowrie. Quite a handful!

Introduction

Wilfred Taylor, for long a popular writer with *The Scotsman*, once described Blairgowrie as 'a garden-embowered town'. The phrase is particularly apt. There are many fine gardens on the slopes of the Hill o' Blair, along the Perth Road and elsewhere. The number increases with every new housing development and of course the heart of the community is not, as in other places, an open square, but a glorious garden, the Wellmeadow. On top of all that, in summertime, shops and houses are adorned with hanging baskets, turning the town into a floral delight.

That, I hope, is how Blairgowrie and Rattray strike the visitor today. In this book we celebrate the town as it used to be: the leisurely streets, solid citizens, sober shop fronts and gleaming interiors. Here is a chance to look again – or for the first time – at buildings that are gone, such as 'the Palace' and the old houses at the Kirkton of Rattray, at workplaces like the mills and the brewery, and to remember one time household names like P.J. Robertson and Paul the Draper.

We have been lucky that earlier this century there were men who were able to record all this. D.G. Monair, the Irish-born photographer and journalist, diligently captured people and events with his camera, bringing an artist's eye to all his work. D. Wilson Laing and his son David followed in Monair's steps, and throughout his life Douglas Davidson has made it his business to collect and cherish pictures from our past.

What we didn't have, when it was most needed, was an amenity group pledged to preserving the best of the old. Such a body might have ensured that Blairgowrie's High Street today wore a more elegant face, that Rattray's Mission Hall still stood. But fortunately, we can now boast an enlightened Community Council and vigorous Civic Trust, both working to maintain the town's character and improve its appearance, while members of the Local History Trust research our past and conserve its artefacts.

Those who grew up in Blairgowrie, as I did, can relish memories revived by these old scenes. I hope that newcomers and strangers will also find the book enjoyable. It may help them a little to understand how and why the town has developed as it has, what it has lost and what it has gained. Above all, I hope the pictures convey something of the flavour of a decent, working Perthshire town.

So now, turn the magic key and step back with me into the pages of yesterday.

Maurice Fleming
Blairgowrie,
August 1997

St Mary's Parish Church on Reform Street was opened in 1885. The last service took place in 1968 and the congregation was then united with the South Church along the street. The building was demolished in 1973 and replaced by St Mary's Court development.

AERIAL VIEW OF BLAIRGOWRIE

This aerial shot from the twenties shows the complex of industrial buildings up-river from the Brig o' Blair. Opposite, the Riverside Drive has not yet been developed and the open ground, bottom right, later became the site of housing developments and the Regal Cinema. At the bottom left of the picture, a railway engine is just leaving Blairgowrie Station. The old Brig itself has been improved twice this century. Some people regretted the loss of the closed parapets which, they thought, had been a lot less draughty than the new open railings! The original bridge was built in 1777 to replace the rowing boat ferry service between Blairgowrie and Rattray.

The Regal Cinema, right, was opened in July 1938 as a rival to Quinn's Picture House in Reform Street. The opening ceremony was performed by Sir Douglas Ramsay of Banff, who complimented the cinema on having 'not a piece of foreign workmanship in the whole building'! The first film shown was *The Singing Marine* starring Dick Powell. Afterwards over 200 of the audience were guests of the directors at a supper in the Queen's Hotel. The Regal later became a bingo hall and was then demolished and replaced by flats in the mid-1990s.

Blairgowrie Cottage Hospital will celebrate its centenary in 2001. The original simple structure has had various extensions and additions. These pillars were re-erected further down Ann Street when the entrance was moved.

John Fleming Junior, The Cross, was one of several 'high class grocers' serving the town in the 1930s. The premises are currently occupied by Thresher's. Other businesses at the Cross have included Black the chemist's and, on the other side, James Ward's newsagent and bookshop and McLeish's fishmonger and poulterer.

P. J. Robertson's was at 61 High Street. The proprietor, Pat Robertson, is pictured with his daughter, Patsy, and a young assistant, David Patience. The premises now house an opticians.

Robertson was a grocer and wine merchant and here he is, left, presiding over his gleaming set of scales. In the foreground is the top of a chair provided for the use of customers (we could do with a few at the checkout points in today's supermarkets!) Does anyone know the names of the dutiful assistants?

HIGH STREET, BLAIRGOWRIE.

B.4603.

This area of the High Street, looking towards The Cross, has seen a number of changes. The Queen's Hotel is now flats, while Tesco's supermarket has replaced the Co-op. The red sandstone house alongside was the home of Dr Shaw who for many years made his calls by chauffeur-driven car. Keiller's Restaurant is now Boots the Chemists. Keiller's bakery was on the ground floor and the restaurant was upstairs.

In its heyday, Gunn's Queen's Hotel was a coaching inn of some splendour. An advertisement in a local town guide from early this century describes it as 'Under Royal Patronage' and 'Patronised by the Elite'. It promised that 'Omnibuses and Porters meet all trains'. The building has recently been converted into flats.

There were several springs or wells on the flat ground known as the Wellmeadow. St Ninian is said to have camped here on an evangelical expedition from Galloway. Later it was a resting place for drovers and their herds. In 1824 the practice of holding fairs and markets on it began, including the famous Fair o' Blair, an annual event in July. The attractive vernacular buildings to the right have long since gone.

The Bank Buildings, Wellmeadow, decorated for King Edward VII's visit to Blairgowrie and Rattray in September 1908. Public toilets have replaced the lean-to shed and house on the left.

This view is barely recognisable as the corner of the Wellmeadow and what is now Lower Mill Street. The two all but forgotten businesses are William Scott, grocer and wine merchant, and George Halson's tea-rooms and bakery. The decorations were almost certainly for the visit to the town of King Edward in 1908, though these citizens don't look all that wild about it.

FROM A PHOTO] "JOHN." [BY J. D. PETRIE.

The Late "Bell man"

This card is postmarked 1905 so loitering in the Wellmeadow is no new thing! The Macpherson Memorial Fountain was gifted to the town by the Macpherson family in 1893 in memory of Allan Macpherson who, after serving on the legislative council of New South Wales, returned to Blairgowrie and devoted himself to local government work in Perthshire. It was an impressive piece of sculpture but unfortunately it was badly damaged in a traffic accident and never properly repaired. Only the base survives and now stands on a new site within the Wellmeadow garden.

John Maclachlan served his time as a boot and shoemaker, but he was eventually persuaded to follow the family tradition and became bellman and town-crier for Blairgowrie and Rattray. According to the local writer Henry Dryerre, old John spent his time 'proclaiming lost dogs, auction sales, entertainments and anything else wanted of him for over half a century'. Does anyone know where his bell is now?

The Lansdowne Golf Club was founded at Rosemount in 1889 and this card from early this century shows the early pavilion. The house on the left, once a tearoom, is still on the far side of Golf Course Road, although it now looks across to today's car park and clubhouse.

SNOWSTORM AT OPENING OF BLAIRGOWRIE BOWLING GREEN. 23/4/08. D. G. M.

The snow had to be cleared from Blairgowrie Bowling Green before the annual opening match could begin in April 1908. Only a few ends had been played when it snowed again. Hailstones drove the players into the pavilion where, according to *The Blairgowrie Advertiser*, 'they found an enjoyable tea'. The report goes on to say, 'It was no easy matter searching for the bowls among (sic) the snow after the storm cleared off'.

Porter staff of Blairgowrie Railway station. Its opening in 1855 was a huge boost to trade in the town and many will remember from the late 1950s the 'Raspberry Special', which took raspberries from all the fruit-growing towns of Perthshire to Covent Garden in London. When the station was demolished in 1982, the clock was rescued by Blairgowrie, Rattray and District Civic Trust and it remains in their safekeeping. It is hoped that the clock one day will again tell the time for citizens of the town from another site.

RAILWAY SMASH AT BLAIRGOWRIE.
19-12-06.

Local photographer D. G. Monair was quickly on the spot when a goods train jumped the points as it passed the signal box at Blairgowrie Station in the winter of 1906. Ten waggons were derailed, two of them almost totally wrecked. However, no one was hurt and a large jar of whisky remained intact!

Blairgowrie has suffered freak storms on three occasions over the last 150 years. There was the Great Storm of 1847 which threw down two arches of the old Brig; and in August 1910, spectators lined the Brig all day to watch the debris of a night of violent rainfall tumbling by – trees, bushes, bits of sheds and even farmyard fowls. Half of the wooden croy which diverted water into the mill lade above the Bridge was washed away on this occasion. After what was described as a 'terrific storm', flooding in the district in 1920 was worse than on these previous occasions. From the Alyth Road the strath looked like a huge loch, with thousands of acres under water. The intrepid D. G. Monair took this picture at the Boatman's House, Coupar Grange, where the occupants were about to be rescued by boat.

George Street after a heavy snow storm. Notice how the pavements have been given priority – would that they were cleared so thoroughly today! Craigie the Slaters' business was round the corner in David Street and the first house on the left was for long their family home.

By the time this picture was taken 'The Palace' had come down in the world, but it is not difficult to imagine what a fine townhouse it must have been. Tradition has it that Prince Charles, the Young Pretender, slept here when passing through. Its site on the south side of the High Street is now occupied by the Co-op.

The original J. B. Greive drapery shop on the High Street. This building was taken down and replaced by new premises for the business.

The splendid interior of Greive's 'new' shop with its elegant fittings and tempting lines in ladies' attire. The picture was taken in 1910. Although changes have been made, inside and out, the windows and door are still recognisable in Doig's store of today.

There seem to be more parents than pupils at this celebration outside Blairgowrie High School, as it used to be known. Empire Day was the name given to Queen Victoria's birthday, 24 May. Long before the new High School arose on Beeches Road, local children received all their primary and secondary education in this one building. Opened in 1879, it had a second storey added in 1909. Today, as Hill Primary, the building still soldiers on.

Allan Street, Blairgowrie.

The businesses in this picture of Allan Street that can be identified are James Richardson's tea-rooms, left, and William Low, grocer, while on the corner, right, is C. Scott and Son, tailors. Low's chain of small shops grew into the supermarket giant which was eventually taken over by Tesco.

Many will remember Robert Cargill's grocer's shop on the corner of Leslie Street and Allan Street. Next to it is another once familiar name, William Smith, the butcher. Smith's was one of four well-patronised butcher's shops in the town before the Second World War.

Paul's high class store in Allan Street opened in 1906 and closed with Mr Paul's retirement in 1923. The site is now occupied by the Clydesdale Bank with the Masonic Temple above. Remarkably, the D. E. shoe shop, left, is still in the same premises and also now takes up the adjacent tobacconist's.

The coronation of King George VI and Queen Elizabeth in May 1937 was celebrated locally with a big procession. This royal float is pictured passing up the Wellmeadow in front of the Commercial Bank and Peark's Stores.

THE ERICHT FROM THE BRIG O' BLAIR.   734

The building of textile mills on the Ericht in the nineteenth century changed Blairgowrie from a rural village of handloom weavers into an industrial town. In the 1870s there were as many as ten mills on the river, employing nearly 2,000. The mills processed flax and later, jute. Looking up-river from the Brig o' Blair, this picture shows, furthest away, the Plash Mill and Muckle Mill. The nearest building was the Meal Mill, the last of the group to be demolished around forty years ago.

New Mart. Blairgowrie.

A view over the Ericht and the Haugh Road to the New Mart. During its lifetime the Mart was used regularly for livestock sales but the site now lies under Davie Park Place, MacDonald Crescent and other housing in this corner of Rattray.

Blairgowrie Cricket team ready for action, *c*1930. The Captain (centre) is R. W. Lowe, who was a prominent architect in the town. 'Bert' Lowe was responsible for the design of a number of homes in the town.

According to the writer who posted this card in 1912, this was the Blairgowrie Football Team. They were champions for the season, having defeated Rattray in 'the local Derby'. Although Blairgowrie and Rattray were united as a single burgh in 1928, there is still an element of rivalry between the two communities.

No, these are not old-timers outside the Sheriff's Office watching for the stagecoach to roll into their Wild West town. They are local worthies at Blairgowrie Bowling Club in 1911 and their names were John Strain, John Barbour, John Clark and William Grant.

Members of Ardblair Curling Club on the pond, Muirton Wood, in January 1929. The main figure is Thomas Todd, who lived in Muirton of Ardblair village, and the man on the right was Adam Hill. The pond, and the other close to it, have long been overgrown and unfit for curling although the trees seen here still stand.

At the Muirton, Blairgowrie.

Mr Brough ('Old Burroch') and his wife outside their fairytale house at Muirton of Ardblair, the woodland village of thatched cottages on the Ardblair estate. The curved treetrunk stretching up to the chimney on the right seems to be some sort of prop. This was one of a number of thatched cottages at the Muirton village which lingered on into this century but of this house only a few stones show where it stood. Muirton was at one time a community of weavers, every family owning their own loom.

Two old worthies of Muirton. Left, Mrs William Gow, who lived to 102; and right, 'Ease Chaipel', who worked for the Gows on their pendicle. No one seems to know what her real name was although it is thought it may have been Isobel. She is standing in the doorway of the Gows' cottage, one of two adjoining cottages now reduced to low walls. Although the thatched cottages have now gone, they were recorded by local photographers and painted by artists such as William Geddes and his son Ewan. Geddes senior had a studio in Blairgowrie.

M. Wilcox Balmoral Road. New Rattray.

Today's residents of Balmoral Road, New Rattray, must wish that the street was as traffic-free as this. It was evidently a good summer when this picture was taken, judging from the stock of sunhats at Stewart the Draper's on the corner of the High Street. In a strict sense Old and New Rattray could be considered as two separate villages but both owed their development to the flax-spinning mills which were opened in the nineteenth century. Those not working in the mills supported themselves by weaving coarse linen fabrics for Dundee manufacturers.

The Square, Old Rattray, Blairgowrie.

722.

Although the postcard publisher called this The Square, Old Rattray, it has long been known as The Cross. The 1920s picture shows the bairns heading home from school. Only the building seen through the gap ahead still stands. The beadle and grave-digger of Rattray Parish Church, Mr Hovelsroud, used to sit on Sim's window-sill while awaiting the arrival of a funeral.

Older Rattray folk will have happy memories of hymns and games in the Mission Hall, right, in Old Rattray High Street. Despite efforts to save it for the community, it was 'dinged doun' over thirty years ago.

How many ministers are honoured today by having their heads put on postcards? The Rev. Thomas Tully, M.A., a native of Fochabers, was minister of Rattray United Free Church at the start of the century, having first come to Rattray in 1894. A good-sized building, it was pulled down early this century.

This was the Craighall Bridge on the main Braemar road until shortly before the Second World War when it was replaced. It had been used since the early nineteenth century when the new route from Blairgowrie to Braemar replaced the Old Military Road over Cochrage Moor.

BLACKCRAIG, 16TH SEPT. 1893. (MR GLADSTONE, SECOND FROM RIGHT.) 19576. J.V.

The Liberal prime minister, William Gladstone, was a guest at Blackcraig Castle, Strathardle, when this rather uncomfortable-looking picnic took place in 1893. The previous year, at the age of 82, he had formed his fourth government. He was to retire from office in 1894. Queen Victoria called him, in her diary, 'wild and incomprehensible' and judging from his expression perhaps one can see why.

A (rather stiff) group in the grounds of Blairgowrie House in 1881. The house was built by Colonel Allan Macpherson about 1790. Seated on the left is the present Sir William's grandfather, William Charles Macpherson. He was probably home on leave from the Indian Civil Service. His wife-to-be, Frances Kinloch, is on the right. The child on the left is probably William's youngest sister, Frances, for whom Embden House in Newton Street was built. Part of Blairgowrie House survives, hemmed in by modern homes off the Coupar Angus Road.

ROSEMOUNT

ROSEMOUNT GATES. No. 27.

Rosemount station was the only stop on the line, pioneered by the Scottish Midland Junction Railway, linking Blairgowrie and Coupar Angus and opened in 1855. A generous financial offer by the company and Allan Macpherson induced some Dundee businessmen to build houses in the area and travel to work by train on the railway line between Blairgowrie and Coupar Angus. After a century's service the station closed although the house still stands.

ESSENDY FRUIT FARM, BLAIRGOWRIE.

'The Tin City' is famous in Blairgowrie folklore. This was a collection of huts built by a group of Essendy fruit-farmers for the pickers who came to harvest the raspberry crop. For many of the pickers it was an escape from the city that they looked forward to from one summer to the next.

A typical crowd of fruitpickers, possibly at Essendy. The farm began marketing fruit in 1902 and were soon responsible for much of Blairgowrie's total crop. The workers were employed by agents throughout Scotland and each season around a thousand people descended on the town to live in the Tin City which had amenities such as a restaurant, grocer's shop and post office. A season at Essendy was regarded as a working holiday by the pickers and they contributed towards their accommodation costs. However, the standard of employees was high and before they were taken on, each had to produce a certificate of good character. Previously, farms tended to employ many from the 'tramp class' who were considered as undesirables by the local people. It was to satisfy them that these stringent controls were introduced.

Kinclaven Ferry

Valentine's Series

Before the building of Kinclaven Bridge near Meikleour, the Tay was crossed at this point by ferry. Known as a 'flying bridge', this took the form of a raft or platform which was pulled across by chains.